Author:
Brian Williams studied English at university and has taught in both primary and secondary education. He worked for *Encyclopaedia Britannica* for several years as Editor of Children's Britannica and is now a full-time writer.

Artist:
David Antram was born in Brighton, England, in 1958. He studied at Eastbourne College of Art and then worked in advertising for fifteen years before becoming a full-time artist. He has illustrated many children's non-fiction books.

Series creator:
David Salariya

Editor:
Karen Barker Smith

First edition for North America (including Canada and Mexico), the Philippines, and Puerto Rico published in 2003 by Barron's Educational Series, Inc.
© The Salariya Book Company Ltd 2003

First published in Great Britain in 2003 by Book House, an imprint of
The Salariya Book Company Ltd
25 Marlborough Place, Brighton BN1 1UB

Please visit the Salariya Book Company at:
www.salariya.com
www.book-house.co.uk

All inquiries should be addressed to:
Barron's Educational Series, Inc.
250 Wireless Boulevard
Hauppauge, New York 11788
http://www.barronseduc.com

Library of Congress Catalog Card No.: 2003100670

International Standard Book No.: 0-7641-2592-3

Printed and bound in China.

Printed on paper from sustainable forests.

Faraday

Pioneer of electricity

Written by
Brian Williams

Illustrated by
David Antram

The Explosion Zone

BARRON'S

Contents

Introduction

Can you think of a world without electricity? No electric light at the flick of a switch, no power to heat our homes, cook our food, start our cars, or work our televisions and computers?

When Michael Faraday was born, there was no electricity available as we know it. People wondered why a comb picked up paper, or why lightning started fires. They gasped when inventors showed off machines that made sparks and gave people shocks. Whatever made the sparks was regarded as a mystery, but of no use to anyone – until Faraday came along. He showed how to make electricity and electrical machines. Faraday flicked the switch to turn on the modern world.

What's the attraction?

Michael Faraday was born on September 22, 1791. He was the third child of Margaret and James Faraday, a blacksmith, who moved from the north of England to find work in London the year that Michael was born. The Faradays were religious and went to chapel every Sunday. They were quite poor, but paid a few pennies a week to send Michael to school.

At 13, Michael had to start work. He got a job with a bookbinder near Oxford Street, in London. His boss, George Riebau, often sent him on errands, which enabled him to see the sights of the city. Mr. Riebau soon realized Michael was clever. While the lad was cheerfully glueing covers onto books, he was also reading them. Michael loved learning about science and inventions. He read about electricity in an encyclopedia and that really sparked his imagination!

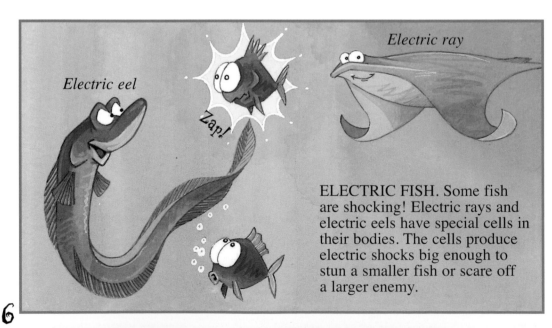

Electric eel

Zap!

Electric ray

ELECTRIC FISH. Some fish are shocking! Electric rays and electric eels have special cells in their bodies. The cells produce electric shocks big enough to stun a smaller fish or scare off a larger enemy.

Rubbing some substances together makes them attract each other...

Here's the science

Mysterious attraction

Over 2,000 years ago, the Ancient Greeks wondered what made a feather stick to a lump of amber. The Greek word for amber was *elektron*. Scientists now know that rubbing the amber with a cloth makes static electricity.

QUICK COMBING CAUSES FRICTION, which moves electrons from your hair to the comb. When the comb has picked up more electrons than protons, it has a negative (-) charge. But your hair now has more protons than electrons, so it has a positive (+) charge. (-) and (+) attract one another, so hair moves toward the comb.

Read all about it

Faraday regularly went to hear science talks. There he made friends with other young people who wanted to learn. Science was all the rage. One day, Faraday was given tickets to lectures by Humphry Davy. Davy was the star scientist of the Royal Institution, a club for people interested in new ideas. His talks were full of "special effects": model volcanoes, colored smoke, and whiffs of "laughing gas" (nitrous oxide) that made people fall over giggling. Faraday made notes and drawings of the lectures and sent them to Davy, asking for a job. In October of 1812 Davy almost blew himself up doing an experiment! He needed an assistant.

IN MARY SHELLEY'S STORY *Frankenstein* (1818), a scientist uses electricity to bring a man-made monster to life. No wonder people were fascinated by tricks with wires and batteries!

NOTEBOOKS. Faraday kept notes and drawings all his life. He thought that experiments could answer most questions in science.

LUIGI GALVANI. In 1771 this Italian scientist observed a dead frog's leg twitch when touched by two different metals. Why? The answer was an electric current.

Sparks fly

Humphry Davy hired Faraday as his assistant. In 1813 they went on a long trip across Europe. Faraday acted as the Davys' servant, but he also met famous people. He talked to André Ampère, a French scientist who knew why electricity travels in a circuit. In Italy, Davy and Faraday visited Alessandro Volta, inventor of the battery. Before Volta, the only way to make electricity was by friction. Friction machines made sparks, which were caught and stored in a glass Leyden jar. No one knew how to create a continuous flow of electric current, enough to light a room or drive a machine. Using Volta's battery, people could do electrical experiments.

Humphry Davy

Michael Faraday

Charge collected by metal comb

Leyden jar

Leather rubbed against glass (friction) makes electric charge

Charge jumps from ball to ball and into the jar

Friction machine (right)

Silver

Zinc

Moist salt-soaked paper

Alessandro Volta

Voltaic pile

How a battery works

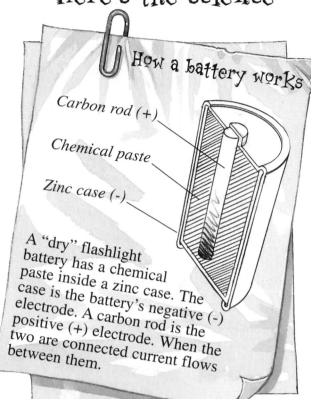

Carbon rod (+)

Chemical paste

Zinc case (-)

A "dry" flashlight battery has a chemical paste inside a zinc case. The case is the battery's negative (-) electrode. A carbon rod is the positive (+) electrode. When the two are connected current flows between them.

Try it yourself

A LEMON BATTERY. Cut two slits in a lemon. Push a copper coin into one and a strip of zinc into the other. Wire the metals up, to make a circuit. The metals react with the acid in the lemon to make a tiny electrical current – enough to light a tiny bulb.

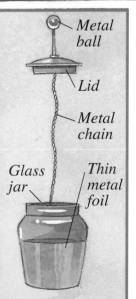

Metal ball

Lid

Metal chain

Glass jar

Thin metal foil

THE VOLTAIC PILE. In Volta's wet battery, pairs of silver and zinc discs were sandwiched between paper or cloth soaked in salt water (above). His battery made electricity from a chemical reaction in this pile of wet discs.

STORING SPARKS. A scientist in the Dutch town of Leyden made the first "Leyden jar" in 1745. It was a glass jar lined with metal foil. Turning a friction machine made static electricity, which jumped into the jar (right). A Leyden jar could store electricity. It was the first type of capacitor.

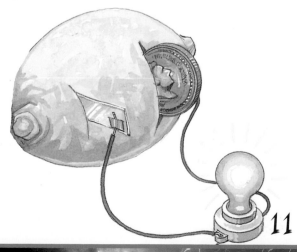

11

Charge!

Davy often left Faraday in charge in their laboratory at the Royal Institution in London. Together, they invented a safety lamp for miners, they did experiments with chemicals, and they blew up things in test tubes! Faraday went to study iron-making in Wales for a while – being a blacksmith's son, he was fascinated by the subject.

In October 1820 Davy rushed in with exciting news. A Danish scientist named Hans Oersted had found a link between magnetism and electricity. He had passed a current along a wire placed close to a magnetic compass and it made the compass needle flicker. This set Faraday wondering – could he use magnets to make electricity?

THE DAVY LAMP. Naked flames were a very dangerous way of lighting coal mines. The new lamp's secret was the metal gauze that cooled the heat from the flame of the burning wick. This stopped the lamp from igniting the methane gas found in mines and so prevented explosions. The safety lamp (opposite) was named after Davy, but in fact Faraday helped him make the first one.

ROOFTOP RESEARCH. One day in 1819 Faraday climbed onto the roof of the Royal Institution to set up an experiment. He tied a wire to a chimney pot and led the wire down to the laboratory. In a thunderstorm, his lightning conductor charged up a Leyden jar with electricity.

It's a miracle! But it's still pretty black in here!

Magnetic poles

The Earth is a magnet. So are some metals. If a bar magnet is hung in the center it will swing until one end points north. The ends, or poles, of a magnet are called North (N) and South (S).

N *(1)* N   S *(2)* N

Opposite poles, N and S, attract one another (2). Like (same) poles, N and N, S and S, repel, or push apart (1).

Hans Oersted

OERSTED'S NEEDLE. Hans Oersted was showing a class of students how electric current from a battery moved along a wire. A compass was lying on the bench close to the wire. Its needle flickered. This showed that an electric current produced a magnetic field.

Metal gauze

Wick

Davy lamp

In a spin

Faraday had other things on his mind, apart from magnets and batteries. In June 1821 he married his sweetheart Sarah Barnard and they lived in rooms in the Royal Institution.

Faraday was asked to write a magazine article on what was known about "electromagnetism" and doing this gave him a new idea. He went back to the laboratory in September 1821 and carefully put together his electrical apparatus: corks, wires, glass jars, mercury, magnets, and Volta-type batteries. He explained, to Sarah and his nephew George, that he was sure an electric current could make a magnetized wire spin. He connected all his bits and pieces to a battery. And, presto! The wire spun around the magnet. George and Faraday danced with glee around the world's first electric motor!

Faraday's first electric motor

Movable magnet

Movable wire

Fixed magnet

Mercury

Battery

It works!

Warning!

NEVER touch liquid mercury – it is extremely toxic to the human nervous system, as well as to fish and animals.

Electric circuit

Bulb

Switch

Battery

Electricity flows only around a circuit. If you break the circuit, you stop the flow of current. That is how a light switch works. Moving the switch one way breaks the circuit (off). Moving it back (on) lets current flow again.

THE FIRST ELECTRIC MOTOR. Two pots of mercury formed part of the electrical circuit (opposite). In each pot was a magnet. When current from the battery passed around the circuit, the "free" wire spun around the fixed magnet.

A SILLY QUARREL. Faraday's discovery made him famous and Humphry Davy became jealous. Davy spread it around that Faraday had stolen ideas from William Wollaston, another scientist. This was untrue.

15

Wired up

The quarrel with Davy upset Faraday and Davy went on treating him like a servant. But Faraday made friends with William Wollaston and received letters of congratulation from Ampère and other scientists. The Faradays lived happily above the laboratory, from which loud bangs, crashes, and flashes could be heard. One loud bang in 1823 signaled another first: Faraday had turned a gas (chlorine) into a liquid. He enjoyed giving lectures at the Royal Institution, where people could exchange ideas. "We light up the house," he wrote cheerfully, in a letter. He was busy doing experiments with coils of wire and magnets. He read how William Sturgeon (in 1825) and American scientist Joseph Henry (in 1829) made electromagnets that could lift heavy weights of iron.

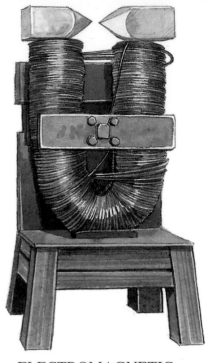

ELECTROMAGNETIC CHAIR. Faraday made electromagnets by winding a long piece of wire around a U-shaped iron bar. This one was so heavy he set it on a chair (above). When the wires were connected to a battery, the iron bar became a magnet.

ELECTROMAGNETS AT WORK. Electromagnets are useful in modern scrapyards. They are hung from the chain of a crane.

When the current is turned on, the electromagnet starts to work. Big ones can pick up old cars. Anything with iron in it is attracted!

DAZZLING DISPLAYS. Faraday's Christmas lectures for children became an annual event. He loved to dazzle his listeners with showers of sparks and glowing arc lamps. One day, children would see electric light in their homes.

Electromagnet coils

A current increases magnetism if the wire it flows along is bent into a loop.

Several loops make a coil. This makes the magnetic effect even stronger.

When a coil is wound around an iron rod and the coil is connected to a circuit, you have an electromagnet! No current means no magnetism.

Switched on

Faraday's Christian religion was an important part of his life and he thought that everything in nature might be connected in unseen ways. Electricity could make magnetism. So could magnetism make an electric current? In August 1831 he proved it.

He wound two long coils of wire onto opposite sides of an iron ring. Then he connected the wires to a compass needle. When he touched the ends of the wire to a battery, the needle flickered. The current seemed to have "jumped." The magnetic field around the first coil had "induced" (started) a current in the second coil. Electromagnetic induction was possible. By October, he had gone on to make a simple generator.

INDUCTION RING. Faraday wound two coils of copper wire (over 120 ft, 36 m, in all) around an iron ring 6 in (15 cm) in diameter. He used twine and calico as insulators. When the current was on, the needle flicked one way. When he switched the current off, the needle flicked the other way!

STAYING LOYAL. In 1827 Faraday was asked to become Professor of Chemistry at London's new university. He politely said no. He preferred to stay at the Royal Institution, which he said had been "a source of knowledge and pleasure for 14 years."

MOVING THE MAGNET. On October 17, 1831, Faraday tried slipping a bar magnet in and out of a coil. Again the compass needle moved! Motion and magnetism: he had found a better way to make, or generate, electricity.

Here's the science

How induction works

Battery

1st coil 2nd coil

Switch

Iron ring Compass needle

Current flowing through the first coil set up an electromagnetic field around it. The magnetism created a short burst of current in the second coil, making the compass needle move. The same thing happened, in the opposite direction, when Faraday turned off the current.

Bar magnet

Compass needle

Coil

A generator

Making electricity to drive machines required energy, Faraday realized. So he harnessed the muscle power of his assistant, Charles Anderson, to turn a wheel and belt machine. The machine made a copper disc spin fast between the poles of a U-shaped magnet. Faraday yelled with delight when he saw the needle move and then stay in its new position. This showed that current was flowing. His spinning disc was a generator. As long as it kept spinning between the poles of the magnet, it would make electricity – one day enough electricity to drive vehicles and factory machines. This was the start of something bigger than even Faraday was aware.

Charles Anderson

First in the field

Faraday was never happier than in the laboratory. While working, he would hop from one foot to the other, rubbing his hands and humming a tune. He was sure now that magnets, static charges, and electric current all produced "fields" of force. He studied the patterns that iron filings made on a card when he placed a magnet near them. In his mind, he saw electromagnetic fields everywhere, invisible as the air in which birds flew and kites soared. The idea of "force-fields" started with Faraday. When Faraday was not working, he enjoyed spending time with his family and went on vacations at the seaside.

CHARLES ANDERSON was a retired army sergeant and an ideal assistant. He never complained, even when kept up all night just because Faraday forgot to tell him to go home!

FARADAY LOVED PLAYING with his nieces and nephews. To amuse them, he built a four-wheeled velocipede (a kind of bicycle) which he rode around Hampstead Heath.

Come and have a go on my velocipede. Pushing the pedals makes it go.

Velocipede

Here's the science

Electromagnetic field

(1)

Iron filings show the presence of a magnetic field. They lie scattered on a card (1) when no current flows through the wire.

(2)

When a current flows, the iron filings make a ring-shaped pattern (2). This shows where the electromagnetic field is.

Lighting up

The generator created by Faraday inspired other inventors to make larger ones, driven by steam engines. He had shown how an electric motor could work, but left others to make the first electric motors for machines. These came in the 1870s, after Faraday's death.

He didn't live to see electric light bulbs either. Faraday knew how a light bulb would work – he had seen thin wires glowing bright and hot when electric current flowed through them. He knew too about arc lamps, invented in 1812, and the first electric lights. They gave a brilliant spark of light, fine for theaters but too bright for reading at home. At night, Faraday worked by gaslight or lit candles. The first light bulbs that worked without burning out or exploding were invented in the 1870s, by Joseph Swan in Britain and by Thomas Edison in America.

Faraday experimenting with an arc lamp

Here's the science

How does a light bulb work?

Filament

Inside a glass light bulb is a thin wire called a filament, surrounded by gas. Thin wire has more resistance to the electrons in electricity than a thick wire. When current flows, the wire gets hot and glows, giving off light.

Filament

Wires carrying current to and from filament

Contact to power supply

FARADAY KEPT WRITING his notebooks, realizing that his memory was fading as he grew older. He created some of the words we still use about electricity, including anode, cathode, and electrode.

Shocking discoveries

n 1839 Faraday fell ill through overwork. When he eventually went back to his research, he tried to use a giant magnet to bend light. He also tried to use sunlight to make electricity. He did not succeed, but his sun power idea was later taken up to produce the photoelectric cell and solar power. He went on testing conductors and insulators. Electricity is dangerous, and Faraday gave himself many burns and electric shocks. He had to find out for himself how to insulate his equipment to control the electric current safely. This meant hours of work, carefully wrapping wires in cloth, twine, or some other material.

Leyden jar

CONDUCTORS. Faraday did experiments with a Leyden jar to find the best conductors (carriers) of electricity. Silver was a good conductor, as was a carrot (being moist). Copper was cheap, so he used copper wire.

FEELING THE STRAIN.
Faraday believed that energy was all around, streaming across the universe. He hoped electricity would unlock the secrets of this universal energy. Sadly, his own energy was failing. He had worked too hard and fell ill. For six years he did little scientific work and was seldom seen in public.

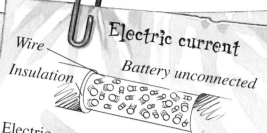

Electric current

Wire

Insulation

Battery unconnected

Electric current is a stream of electrons. Usually, electrons move in different directions. When a battery is connected to a copper wire, it pushes all the electrons in the wire in the same direction. They flow along the wire as current. Insulation around the wire stops electrons from escaping.

Battery connected

Electron

INSULATORS.
To insulate wires, Faraday wrapped them in non-conducting material. He tried leather, parchment, hair, twine, cloth, wood, even feathers. Plastics are good insulators, but there were no plastics in Faraday's time.

LECTURING AGAIN. By the 1850s Britain's most famous scientist was again busy giving lectures. He warned that not enough children were learning science.

DANGER! Do NOT play with electrical wiring!

CAUTION: Use only a small battery (1.5 volts) when doing simple experiments. Any voltage can and will cause burns to skin, large voltage can cause death. Check with a teacher or other adult before working with any electrical current.

27

Glossary

Amber The hard yellowish brown fossilized resin of pine trees, known to the Ancient Greeks as *elektron*.

Arc lamp The electric light, invented by Humphry Davy in 1812, which gives off a bright spark between carbon-tipped wires.

Battery A device for storing electricity that works when metals react chemically with liquids.

Capacitor A device for storing electric charge.

Cells Small units that make up the living tissue of animals and plants; also a chemical device for making electricity.

Charge An amount of electricity.

Chemical reaction A process in which two or more substances combine to make different substances.

Circuit The complete path taken by an electrical current along a suitable conductor.

Conductor A substance that allows electricity to flow through it easily.

Current The flow of electrons along a conductor.

Diameter The measurement of the widest part of a circle.

Electrode A metal or some other conductor that allows electrical current to pass in or out of an electrical device.

Electromagnet A magnet that works only when a current passes through a coil of wire wrapped around an iron core.

Electron The part of an atom that carries a negative (-) electrical charge.

Friction The force that acts on one surface rubbing against another.

Gauze A netlike mesh of wire.

Generator A machine for making electricity from mechanical energy.

Insulator Any material that blocks the flow of electrical current.

Iron filings Tiny pieces of iron, easily affected by a magnet.

Magnetic field The lines of force around the poles of a magnet.

Magnetism The invisible force that attracts some metals and is given out by an electric current as well as by some substances.

Particles The tiny parts inside an atom.

Photoelectric cell A device for turning light into electrical energy.

Pioneer Someone who is among the first to do something.

Proton The part of an atom that carries a positive (+) electrical charge.

Resistance The amount of opposition a material has to the flow of electric current through it.

Solar power Using the sun's rays to produce energy.

Static electricity An electric charge that is not moving.

Steam engine A machine using steam from a heated-water boiler to drive pistons and turn wheels.

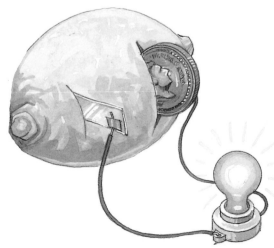

Index